THE LIVING ROCKIES

THE LIVING ROCKIES

G B PUBLISHING

Photographic studies by George Brybycin:

The High Rockies
Colourful Calgary
Our Fragile Wilderness
The Rocky Mountains
Banff National Park
Jasper National Park
Colourful Calgary II
Wildlife in the Rockies
Rocky Mountain Symphony
Enchanted Wilderness
Wilderness Odyssey
Rocky Mountain Symphony II
Romance of the Rockies
Calgary—The Sunshine City
The Living Rockies

Front cover: Kananaskis Country. Opal Range.
Back cover: Indian paintbrush

Text Editor: Stephani Keer
Layout and design: George Brybycin
Printed and bound in Singapore by
Kim Hup Lee Printing Co Pte Limited

First Edition 1989

ISBN 0-919029-12-4   Hard cover

For current list, please write to:
G B PUBLISHING, Box 6292, Station D,
Calgary, Alberta, Canada T2P 2C9

Text and photographs by George Brybycin

Canada Geese (Branta canadensis).

INTRODUCTION

Although beautiful, mysterious and exotic, the name the Rocky Mountain suggest a desolate, desert-like environment. The reality, however, is just the opposite. The Rockies are teeming with rich and varied wildlife. The flora, plants and forests are of extraordinary beauty. Only a small part of this mountain world is a mountain desert, a wasteland. The areas above 2,300 meters are more-or-less lifeless, a realm of ice, snow and craggy-rocky peaks. Yet even there on top of nearly 3,000 meters of mountain, quite often one can observe a hardy mountain dweller, the pika. A few blades of grass, some alpine flowers clinging to a rock is enough for this rabbit-like rodent to survive.

Eagle and falcon build their nests on high ledges of inaccessible mountains. In the lower parts, every square meter of land is inhabited. Invisible at first glance, there are smaller forms of life everywhere. Waters are full of life and in the southwestern Rockies, even a harmless snake can be found.

All native wildlife is well represented here and their chances of survival are very good, thanks to blessed protective status of five Rocky Mountain national parks. Regardless of the quite strong and permanent presence of man in the Rockies, the original inhabitants, the animals, hold their own quite well. Some species are more adaptable to changes than others. The coyote is the most flexible in changing its ways. The goat holds the most conservative reputation. One can see a bald eagle right next to Banff townsite at Vermilion Lakes or an osprey nesting right at the entrance to Waterton Park. Large herds of elk or deer are present throughout the region; the goat and sheep population is healthy and steady. Great moose can be found along the rivers and lakes. In northern parts mountain caribou inhabit the high plateaus and valleys.

The predators, like wolf, wolverine, coyote, fox, cougar, bobcat are ever present but because of their secretive nature of hunter, seldom can be seen. And, of course, the most colourful characters of them all, loved by everybody, the bears provide us with great thrill and excitement.

As the title suggests this album intends to portray a great variety of flora and fauna typical of The Living Rockies.

Delightfully looking but not edible wild mushrooms.

The idyll on the alpine meadow. The mating grizzly bear (Ursus arctos).

Kananaskis Country. Endless forests, flower-carpeted meadows, hiker and naturalist paradise.
On the horizon, Mt. Foch and Sarrail Group.

*Picturesque landscape of The Valley of the Ten Peaks where forests are healthy and the meadows display
all colours of nature's palette. Banff National Park.*

Fed by glacial waters of Wapta Icefield, Hector Lake is one of the most beautiful-unspoiled lakes of the Rockies. Viewed from Bow Peak. Banff National Park.

Tranquil and serene morning along Sunwapta River. Jagged Endless Chain Range in the background.
Jasper National Park.

Clear, life-giving waters of mountain creek rush down the slopes of Mt. Hector.
Banff National Park.

Delicate, eye-pleasing Grass Pink (Dianthus armeria) can be found on western slopes of southern Rockies.

Many species of insects find suitable habitat feeding on a variety of honey-bearing flowers and trees throughout the Rockies.

Commonly found throughout the Rockies, mule deer (Odocoileus hemionus) *doe.*

A majestic moose (Alces alces) *with full-grown antlers in late autumn.*

Known for its incredible beauty and emerald waters, Moraine Lake is nestled in the Valley of the Ten Peaks,
Banff National Park.

High up on the western slopes of Mt. Temple hangs little picturesque Lake Annette,
Paradise Valley, Banff National Park.

Intricate art of a spider, decorated by a morning dew, glitters in bright autumn sun.

Out of 40,000 species of the gastropods, only several species of snail and slugs find the Rockies suitable for home.

Located high in a remote area of Waterton Lakes National Park, Lineham Lake viewed from Mt. Lineham on an early summer morning.

A major Canadian carnivorous predator coyote (Canis latrans),
common in the Rockies.

Most common of all bears, the black bear (Ursus americanus).
This omnivorous predator is well-adapted to the
mountain environment.

The world of its own. Unmatched beauty of mountain lake and its surroundings. Teeming with life, forests and meadows; reaching to the sky, jagged mountains. Echoes from ice avalanches at nearby Wapta Icefield and the whistle of everpresent breeze, wind or storm complete the cacophony of lively sounds of the Rockies. Peyto Lake, Banff National Park.

"To see the world in a drop of water or a seed," wrote a poet. The beauty of a mountain torrent motion and rich decorations created by the first frost.

The humble but pretty dandelion (Taraxacum scopulorum) is ever-present in the Rockies.
This early spring harbinger provides a valuable protein to many mammals,
including just-out-of-hibernation bears.

Silt-filled waters rushing down from Wapta Icefield feed this incredible blue Bow Lake, the water source of the Bow River. Photographed in late autumn from Bow Peak, Banff National Park.

The Valley of the Ten Peaks viewed from the Eiffel Lake trail. Banff National Park. The area, including Larch and Consolation Valleys, houses the most spectacular Larch trees in the Rockies.

Common and sometimes too friendly gray jays (Perisoreus canadensis) of corvidae family are the smallest of the species. Commonly found in northwestern coniferous forests of Canada.

Kananaskis Country. Opal Range. Eastern slopes of Alberta Rockies. One of the most attractive areas in the Canadian Rockies, already gravely endangered by overdevelopment.

Maligne Lake, Jasper National Park. A wild, pristine and naturally beautiful area. A home for moose, deer, caribou, elk, black and grizzly bear and many more species of small wildlife.

A Rocky Mountain bighorn sheep (Ovis canadensis) *ewe with her lamb on high meadows of Kananaskis Country.*

On the western slopes of the British Columbia Rockies, the maple tree is a common sight. The fiery colours of the autumn are well-worth seeing.

Nature, the artist, has created this intricate masterpiece. Delicate morning dew shines like diamonds or pearls on colourful poplar leaves.

Looking northwest from Mt. Foch in Kananaskis Country. Lakes, rivers, many torrents and rich, lush vegetation provide very favourable conditions for a variety of wildlife in the area.

High on slopes of Mt. Carthew, a lone Rocky Mountain sheep (Ovis canadensis) ewe surveys her domain. Waterton Lakes National Park.

North American porcupine (Erethizon dorsatum) can be found throughout the Rockies. Photograph taken at the high meadows of Vermilion Range. Kootenay National Park.

Broad-leaved Willow Herb (Epilobium latifolium). Found in well-watered areas along rivers and high alpine creeks on sandy, gravelled bars. Reaches 30-40 cm. in height. The whole plant is edible and tastes like spinach when boiled.

The splendour of alpine landscape. Vermilion Range, Kootenay National Park. Lush alpine meadows, glaciers, rugged mountains and blue sky above. The area is frequented by the grizzly bear, wolverine, elk, goat, porcupine and many more.

Icy waters of Lake Oesa cheerfully rush down toward Lake O'Hara, Yoho National Park. Odaray Mountain dominates the horizon. The area is, in the opinion of many, the most attractive in the entire Rockies, featuring high mountains, glaciers, emerald lakes, lush forests and meadows.

Looking at Takakkaw Falls, people ask where that water comes from. This picture answers that. Wapta Icefield and its south tongue, Daly Glacier (right), provide all the water. Across the Yoho Valley to the west, the ice-capped The President dominates the horizon. Mt. Niles on the left. Yoho National Park.

Western Anemone (Anemone occidentalis).
This showy, early spring flower can be found
on moist alpine meadows.

Calypso orchid (Calypso bulbosa). Found in lower forests in early summer throughout the Rockies.

Desolate, lifeless at first glance, big rugged Mt. Balfour photographed from Mt. Burgess, Yoho National Park. Actually, this area is blessed with one of the richest flora and fauna in the Rockies. Please note on lower-shadowy part of photo a tiny white ribbon of water, Takakkaw Falls.

A pleasant panorama unfolds when looking north from Bow Peak, Banff National Park. Mt. Murchison, Mt. Silverhorn, Observation Peak and Cirque Peak, below which sits Dolomite Pass and Helen Lake (not visible). In the shadow are these spectacular meadows full of alpine flowers and...grizzlies.

The Valley of the Ten Peaks and Moraine Lake. Banff National Park. Early snow abruptly ended a very short summer.

The confluence of Kicking Horse River and Amiskwi River, Yoho National Park. On horison, Ottertail Range.

Rawson Creek originates at Rawson Lake and flows down to Upper Kananaskis Lake.

A hoary marmots (Marmota ealigata) *at family picnic. Yoho National Park.*

The spectacular wilderness of Mount Robson Provincial Park, Berg Lake and the cascading north slopes of Mt. Robson Berg Glacier.

The agile and fearless acrobat of the heights, mountain goat (Oreamnos americanus) *and kid overlooking Athabasca River, Jasper National Park.*

Brightly lit by the morning sun, Crowfoot Mountain looks on tranquil, crystal-clear Bow Lake, Banff National Park.
Fishing is great and area abounds in wildlife.

Lower Waterfowl Lake surrounded by spectacular, tall peaks is home for rich wildlife.
Moose and loon are most visible, Banff National Park.

The Ramparts, Amethyst Lakes, Astoria River, all located in spectacular Tonquin Valley, Jasper National Park.
The area is home for large herds of mountain caribou, moose, grizzly bear, goat,
marmot, porcupine, pika and small rodents.

Red Monkey Flower (Mimulus lewisii). *This spectacular perennial alpine flower grows in British Columbia and Alberta's southerly Rockies.*

Glacier Lily (Erythronium grandiflorum). *This showy, bright yellow flower, common in most North American mountains, flourishes by alpine brooks and moist meadows.*

Mirror-like Witney Lake and Yellowhead Mountain just west of Jasper. Mount Robson Provincial Park.

Widely recognized guardian of the Bow River, Castle Mountain is reflected in Copper Pond. Banff National Park.

Wintery Wapta Icefield and surrounding forest by Bow Lake, Banff National Park. An excellent x-country and touring ski terrain.

Easily adaptable to any environment, an intelligent and efficient hunter coyote (Canis latrans) *tries to cross half-frozen Bow River, Banff National Park.*

Annual autumn show of spectacular colours at Larch Valley, above Moraine Lake, attracts thousands of visitors, Banff National Park.

After forest fire at Vermilion Pass, Kootenay National Park. New plant life attracts moose and scores of other animals.

A bumper crop of Wild Rose (Rosa woodsii) *chips.*

Lush green forest floor of British Columbia Rockies.

Sunwapta River near its source, Columbia Icefield, Jasper National Park.

Emerald Lake and a new day witnessed from the summit of Mt. Burgess, Yoho National Park.

Mirror-like, still waters of Consolation Lake. Glacier and north face of Mt. Quadra in the background, Banff National Park.

Artistry of first frost along mountain torrent.

Yet another emerald jewel of the Rockies, a small lake just below Lake Oesa. Yoho National Park.

Three young elks (Cervus elaphus) *resting at the forest edge on a warm summer day. Jasper National Park.*

Autumn displays its best in colour along Athabasca River near Japser, Jasper National Park.

Rocky Mountain sheep (Ovis canadensis) *ewe with a yearling.*

Two Rocky Mountain sheep (Ovis canadensis) *lambs in different colour phases.*

Spectacular mountains, shining snowcaps, glittering silver ridges, deep mysterious murky waters. Jagged peaks gently aglow in last rays of the setting sun. A long late autumn night falls over Maligne Lake, Jasper National Park.

A place of exceptional beauty and charm but, at the same time, rugged, wild and dangerous. The possibility of rock or ice avalanche is ever present. Lake Oesa, Yoho National Park.

Next to overdeveloped Lake Louise, yet tranquil and full of magic wilderness. Mt. Fairview, coniferous forest and friendly gray jay makes the hike a pleasure. Banff National Park.

Incredible clarity and colour of the water and the surroundings of rich, healthy forests and meadows makes Lake O'Hara and the area a very attractive tourist destination. So much so that access to the area is being controlled and camping strictly regulated to prevent overuse of this fragile environment.

Moraine Lake, Banff National Park. Fifty years ago it must have been a very pristine, naturally wild and serene place. Today, thousands of people visit the area every day with their dogs, cats, picnic baskets, beer bottles and other "necessities." Unfortunately, some of them are not environmentally conscious.

Humble spring harbinger—Prairis Crocus (Anemone patens). A plant native to the Prairies, Foothills and lower mountains.

At home in the Rockies, elk or Wapiti (Cervus elaphus) spends summer in the forest or meadow, while wintering in lower valleys.

Wintery Bow River and Three Sisters just east of Canmore.

Wapta Falls on Kicking Horse River, Yoho National Park.

It is hard to realize how clear a mountain lake can be, until one sees it. Lower Consolation Lake,
Banff National Park.

Extinct in the wild, a few reservations are maintained to keep Buffalo or American bison (Bison bison) alive.
Buffalo Paddock near Waterton Lakes National Park.

Picturesque Herbert Lake, Banff National Park.

Mule deer (Odocoileus hemionus).   *Canada goose* (Branta canadensis).

Consolation Lake and squat pyramid of Mt. Temple, Banff National Park.

Mt. Kidd reflected in a mountain pond along Kananaskis River. Kananaskis Country.

Vermilion Pass, Kootenay National Park. A lightning-caused forest fire has burned a large area of wilderness here. New plant life and, with it, new fauna flourishes here. Take a walk along a nature trail and you will be amused how beneficial fire can be to the forest. Nutrition from ashes and decaying logs and plenty of light allow plants which otherwise would not grow here to do very well. What will happen when this new forest grows big and tall? Some of these sun-loving forest floor plants will die, some will survive on sunny slopes and clearings. Nature knows best how to manage itself; nature is eternal.

The glory of the heights, alpine meadows, carpets of flowers and plants. Thanks to national park status, some parts of our wilderness remain intact from destructive development. Kootenay National Park.

The Valley of the Ten Peaks, Banff National Park, viewed from Eiffel Lake trail. Regardless of strong human presence, grizzly bear might be seen in the area in early summer or late autumn.

Early summer in high mountains, large snow patches cover the land in July. Ptarmigan Lake viewed from Fossil Mountain, Banff National Park. The area is permanent home to the grizzly bear.

First-hand proof that grizzlies like to have a splash on a hot summer day. This young adult was all by himself and acted very inquisitive toward the author.

Bear Grass (Xerophyllum tenax). *This perennial showy, exceeding one-meter-in-height plant favours dry, sunny, subalpine clearings and meadows. Waterton Lakes National Park is its Alberta northern limit. In British Columbia, Bear Grass can be found further north because of milder climate.*

The Ramparts, Amethyst Lakes at Tonquin Valley, Jasper National Park. This remote valley attracts a relatively large number of visitors but sustains a quite-undisturbed, healthy ecosystem. Mountain caribou (Rangifer tarandus montanus) *inhabit the area as well as grizzly, wolf, moose and a number of smaller mammals.*

Mt. Rundle on the left and Sulphur Mountain by Banff townsite, viewed from the slopes of Mt. Norquay,
Banff National Park.

Kinney Lake and Whitehorn Mountain. Abundance of lush flora and variety of fauna can be enjoyed in Mount Robson Provincial Park.

Maligne Lake, Jasper National Park. This area is blessed with incredible beauty, wildlife and the peace.

The Great Blue Heron (Ardea herodias). *This stately bird hunts by day or night, stalking its prey in the shallows with great patience.*

Oregon grapes (Berberis repens). *Dwarf, creeping shrub bearing berry-like fruit is found in Waterton Lakes National Park and commonly in British Columbia.*

Proverbial carpets of flowers can be admired in August in Helen Lake area. This ice-capped giant on the right is Mt. Hector, Banff National Park.

Eye-pleasing red Bunchberry (Cornus canadensis) *finds the tree trunk a hospitable place to live.*

Steller's Jay (Cyanocitta stelleri).　　　　*Clark's Nutcracker* (Nucifraga columbiana).

Fraser River, Overlander Falls, Mount Robson Provincial Park. Kayaker is just about to negotiate the dangerous falls.

Submerging kayaker does not realize that he is heading for near tragedy.

After 62 long seconds under the water, kayaker emerges from the murky whirlpool.

To celebrate friend's survival, kayakers jump to the icy, dangerous water.

Delicious and pretty Wild Strawberry (Fragaria glauca) *common throughout the Rockies.*

Wilderness awakens at early daybreak or even earlier. The time of the year does not matter: Daybreak is the time. The predatory law of the hunter and hunted dictates that. Most predation occurs at daybreak, so no one wants to be surprised or take a chance. All wake up and play that eternal game of survival hide-and-seek. Because many predators also hunt nocturnally, the hunted practically never really sleep. Most animals nap and doze off a lot, except those who do not have predators, like bears or rodents in the safety of their burrows. A carnivore's life depends on another animal's death. For them, to kill is to live and this is nature's law.

One early summer morning, I walked along a mountain trail and suddenly noticed a commotion on the meadow. I froze and watched. In the tall grass, an animal chased something I could not see, all over the meadow. At first, it looked like a red fox but finally the hunter turned out to be a coyote. Judging by the speed at which the coyote moved, the prey must have been quite large and fast, a hare, I thought. The chase continued for a while and then all stopped. I walked cautiously toward the scene of the hunt and what did I see? The coyote lying down on his back with all four feet up, holding his nose with his front feet. I was only five meters away and saw the coyote's nose was bleeding profusely. It was suffering so much that it could not detect my presence or just did not care. After a while, the coyote got up, looked at me without great concern and, still dizzy and wobbling, trotted past me toward his "breakfast." I moved forward and frightened him off. On the flowery meadow lay in death a large white weasel. I examined the agile victim and then backed off a bit. The rightful owner, without delay, consumed his meal in a few seconds. I noticed his still-bleeding nose had a chunk of flesh missing. I was very relieved to realize that my sandwiches were in my knapsack and I just bought them without getting my nose bloody.

Two or three years later, I drove a car nearby that area in late winter. The winter was very cold and extremely snowy. Movement caught my eye and I noticed a coyote. I stopped, camera at the ready, and waited. I could not believe it. The coyote, like a domestic pet dog, came right to my car, put his feet at the door and his yellow intelligent eyes said: "Please, would you help me? I am nearly starved to death. The winter was long, tough and life was very rough. Please."

I looked at that desperate creature and unmistakably recognized him by the missing part of his nose. That was the weasel hunter.

"Now," I said, "sorry pal, but National Park rules forbid feeding wildlife. Survival-of-the fittest is the law that governs here and I never, ever break the law and feed wildlife."

The coyote would not take my explanation for an answer. I looked at him again and saw ribs and bones covered with skin. Sorry that I could not help, the creature's trust in a human and these desperate eyes that I will never forget, melted my heart and I decided to help. All I had in my car was half-a-box of assorted cookies. They were gone as soon as he could get them. I'm sorry I did this, but that was a genuine humane response to a creature's misery and suffering. After that I drove away immediately, because his still-hungry eyes asked for more and I did not have anything to give. You're welcome, pal, I thought when driving away. If I have saved your life, that makes me more humane and fulfilled. Hope to see you on the trail in better times.

While hiking up the Hoodoo trail in Yoho National Park, I decided to continue a bit higher past the Hoodoos following a narrow game trail toward Vaux-Cancellor Col. Soon I noticed signs of disturbance on the ground. Something has happened here, I thought. Long white hair was scattered; the soil and vegetation disturbed. The signs continued down the slope. At one spot, I noticed a lot more hair and a large pile of half digested cud. Continuing down a steep slope, 20 meters further by the creek, the whole mystery was solved. A bare skeleton of a goat rested peacefully on mountain Avens meadow. The bones still were covered with meat here and there, and the front legs from the knee down were intact. I knew the predator was around, that it would eventually finish the feast, eating to the last bone. Nothing is wasted in nature. Looking nervously around, I took a series of photographs of "the scene of the crime" and retraced my steps, analysing everything again. The first signs of the fight were on the trail right under a large pine tree. Who had done it? Black bear seldom kill, but eat already killed carcasses; grizzly could not catch an agile goat on a steep terrain. A cougar is the prime suspect. It sat at the tree and when the goat came along, it jumped and after a considerable struggle, killed the goat. The next day, I went to see what had happened overnight. Many bones had been eaten up, the front legs cleaned up of meat and a part of the jaw was missing.

Salt lick is the place where animals gather mostly at dusk and dawn. When there is a prey, there is a predator waiting ready to strike. In Mount Robson Provincial Park on the Kinney Lake trail I quite often have seen moose, deer, elk sipping salty water near Knowlton Falls. One day, I was going to climb around Robson Glacier so I started very early. When I reached the salt lick, it was still dark. I sat quietly behind the tree and waited. There were some animals down there but I could not see them. All sorts of sounds and voices could be heard during that time but nothing unusual happened. Suddenly, a loud noise came from beind me, coming straight toward me. A loud rumble, broken branches and a great tumult passed right next to me.

In the vague, early dawn, I recognized a big, great bull moose. He went down to the salt lick to join three others of his specie. I waited for the next ten minutes and then continued up the trail. Very soon, on one of these trail's sharp bends along the Robson River, I was suddenly next to a cougar sitting and looking down the river. The early twilight and the noise of cascading water prevented the cat from seeing or hearing me. Here is a big predator only ten meters away and I pondered what to do. Take a picture, I thought; too dark. Then look and absorb all the danger, beauty and pleasure of the encounter. I clung tightly to my ice-axe and just looked and enjoyed. Amazingly, for several minutes, the cat never took his eyes off that water. Was there a salmon coming up, or perhaps a beaver? The big cat certainly was looking at something very attentively. Since the cat was in my way, after delighting myself watching, I had to let him know I was here and that I wanted to pass by, no harm, pal. I curled my hand around my mouth and said yahooo! In the now-better light, I could see in the cat's eyes fear and wild defiance. Instantly, the cat turned towards me in that typical ready-to-jump posture of predators. I do not know how long it lasted but seemed like ages. Goose pimples covered my entire body, but I kept staring straight at him. The cat evaluated the situation for a while

motionless, and then jumped right across the trail, reaching the escarpment in one long leap and all I could see was that long, heavy tail wagging through the bush, an incredible sight. On the other side of the river, a moose was browsing along the shore undisturbed. The cougar would have no chance to bring down a large moose, so he just watched and waited for something else to come along. On another occasion, when I climbed the southwest slopes of Mt. Robson nearby, I found a front leg of a goat. It appeared the cougar had no problem finding a decent meal.

Camping out a lot, one has to encounter all sort of creatures which are harmless but pure nuisances to us humans. Mice, squirrel, pika and marmot came to mind. Years back, when Mary Wright ran the lodge at Berg Lake in Robson Park, the area attracted all sort of wild creatures because the food associated with people was there. Mary, in her sixties then, assured me, however, that "in all these years, I have never heard of bears around here." The next morning, I ran into a bear just next to the lodge. When the parks people took down the lodge and built on its spot a day use shelter, all these creatures were deprived of their source of food, and thus became very aggressive and cunning. Going up there for a few days of camping in bear country creates a real problem with food storage. There is no safe place in the wilderness to store food, unless you carry a steel container. At that time, the shelter had a steel wire span across the ceiling. I hung my food bag up there for the night. Next morning, I found a hole in the bag and all the stuff messed up, with only a few items wrapped in heavy foil intact. The next day, I suspended the food bag on a very fine wire from the v-shaped, steep ceiling. The same thing happened.

At the Bow Hut by Wapta Icefield, legend has it that Leo the rat will bite off your foot while you sleep, never mind eating all of your food. One day, I arrived at the hut, started cooking my meal and, to my disbelief, that legendary Leo was real and already munching on my crackers in bright daylight. As quickly as he appeared, he just vanished after my disapproval of his behaviour. After checking the cabin, I discovered a hole in the wall 10 cm. across, so Leo was a fair-sized pack rat. Later on, more people arrived, and a few frustrated guys attempted to kill Leo when the rat jumped unceremoniously at their food, but Leo laughed them off. He survived many attempts on his life and knew how to handle his own security.

All night, Leo feasted, chewed and munched on everything he could find, including my boots.

While climbing up to Abbot Pass from the south, on a very snowy November day, I noticed a single animal track going up. I crisscrossed it many times and it ended up by the hut. All night, I heard noises in the hut, but I attributed that to the ghosts who live in most huts. Next morning, however, I came face to face with a very pretty "ghost"—a large, black martin in the kitchen. It took me a while to evict this unregistered guest. I never heard from him again, which means he entered the hut through the open doors. There was no hole in the floor or wall. I had a similar encounter with a martin or fisher at the Bryant Creek Hut. I do not want to bore you with more mice stories, but two of my vans had no screen in the fresh air vents and as a result, I slept many, many nights with mice crawling over my face, getting into my sleeping bag and eating all my food. Thanks, GM.

When one looks at our National Parks today and twenty years ago, one notices that development has increased quite drastically. The parks were created to preserve pristine, natural areas as they were and protect them from human intrusion. The charter of the National Parks is being violated bit by bit, year by year. Here a little hotel or restaurant, there a ski lift or parking lot and so on and on. Obviously, the millions of visitors need services, but it could be worked out to the parks' benefit with all major services located outside the park. Within the park, there would be only an information centre and very essential services. Kootenay and Yoho Parks are like that and visitors love them. After all, people come here from crowded, polluted, noisy cities to see unspoiled, real wilderness. The ideal solution is found in Denali National Park in Alaska, where one can get in only by shuttle bus. There is not one single commercial outlet in the park. Now, *that* is a real park.

An experiment was conducted in Europe to save some mountain lakes from overuse and destruction. There was a lodge and road right to the lake. Every day, 5,000 people visited the area. One day, the lodge was taken down, the road removed and land relandscaped to its natural state, and whoever wants to see the lake must hike up one kilometer from the parking lot. The visitor rate has dropped to 2,000 per day. No garbage, no noise and no abuse. The lake is recovering nicely from nearly total destruction. Moraine Lake came to mind immediately. Speaking of Moraine Lake, every time I go there, I see hordes of people with children throwing rocks at that still-beautiful emerald water. In a National Park, you are not supposed to touch anything. It is very clear to me that if this mindless trend continues, there will be no lake one day. Is that why, by Lake Louise, there are these ugly, man-arranged boulders along the shores? Yes. Some people just cannot behave like civilized, educated and considerate beings. Nearby, Consolation Lake is as beautiful as Moraine Lake, but because one must walk two kilometers from the car, only a few people get there.

One early morning, I hiked up to Consolation Lake, hoping to see a moose or a grizzly frequenting the area. The sun came up, and created a paradise of light and colour. I photographed gorgeous reflections in that incredibly clear water and then sat by the water, absorbing the breath-taking scenery, peace and seclusion. A porcupine came right to me to investigate who I was or just to say hello; several ducks majestically glided through that mirror-like water (plate 82). The real unsurpassed paradise, I thought. Suddenly, all that magic was gone. From behind a frontal moraine, a group of people emerged, screaming, yelling and roaring. When they reached the lake, all six of them started throwing rocks into that peaceful, green water. They walked by the other side of the lake and kept throwing rocks until disappearing behind boulders at the far end. The magic gone, my day ruined, I just left the area anticipating more people to come. On the way down, I pondered what makes people so inconsiderate or just plain ignorant. The National Park charter very clearly stipulates that, to protect the parks areas, we must leave them unimpaired, undisturbed, for future generations. What does it mean? You do not pick the flowers, plants, rocks or anything else. Take only photographs and unforgettable memories and leave only footprints on the trail. I have many times witnessed people chopping a tree in a National Park to build a fire, and camp anywhere they please, leaving all the garbage behind. All that garbage weighs only ounces. Why not take it down with you and keep the wilderness wild and undisturbed? It is surprising to see travel and tour brochures so often showing pictures of people feeding animals in a National Park as a fun thing to do. As a result, some people stop a car in front of a bear and try to photograph themselves with the bear, or better yet, hug a bear. Many people have been injured, even killed, because of that. Out of the dozens of bear stories, I remember one very vividly. There was a bear jam on the Jasper highway, bears visited every car and many people responded with food. A new car arrived, a bear approached, and the tourists rolled down the window and hand fed the bear. On the back seat there was a small dog, very excited and nervous about the bear. The dog's growling and barking made the bear nervous and agitated, finally, the dog barked loudly and in a threatening manner. One whack by the bear and there was a wet spot left on the seat. The dog died instantly. The people rolled up the window and took off immediately, hopefully learning a lesson. Luckily, it was only a dog this time.

It was the end of April and winter at its best at Floe Lake, Kootenay National Park. Solo as usual, I went on skis for an overnight stay. It was an uneventful trip and I reached Numa Pass in five hours. Not a soul around, immense snow coverage and the winter landscape looked so peaceful and glorious. The sky was overcast and the temperature quite civilized. I pitched my tent in a quiet, sheltered gully, had a small meal and, later on when the weather improved, I climbed up a small ridge above the pass to take photographs. When I reached the top, a wind gust blew that virgin, fluffy snow and I could see nothing. It was like being in the middle of the Columbia Icefields in a whiteout situation. After a while, when the wind picked up strength, I realized that I might be in trouble. I lost all sense of direction and couldn't figure out which way my tent was. The wind kept blowing, visibility was gone for good and nightfall was around the corner. I was dressed well but not to be outside for very long. I tried not to panic or do something irrational. I tried to go in circles but not too far away. The tent was only 200 meters away but which way? I was getting a bit cold and quite nervous. If that blizzard didn't stop and night came, I would freeze very quickly, I thought. The strong wind obliterated my track and I could not retrace my way. Miraculously, the wind slowed down just minutes before nightfall and I could see some landmarks and navigate myself towards the well-hidden gully camp. One more lesson learned, one more dangerous close call survived. How long will luck be with me? The night was peaceful and quite comfortable. Unfortunately, the next day was overcast as well. I did not produce any quality photographs and nearly lost my life. A tough business to be in. Down the trail I noticed a porcupine feeding on the willow bark. I took a few pictures, not coming any closer to porky than a ski pole.

On the way down, I felt a nagging pain in my right arm by the elbow, but ignored it. Pain is nothing new to me. When I reached the car and took off my jacket, I felt a strong pain by the elbow again. To my dismay, there was a quill sticking out of my heavy sweater. Well, we have all heard these old wive's tales that a porcupine shoots its quills at an attacker. No tales any more; at least for me. This is a science from now on. The quill went through my jacket, sweater and shirt so deep to my arm that I was unable to pull it out. Fearing that it might break, I left it and drove home. Here, I took tongs and gently but with difficulty pulled it out, and squeezed out the blood to prevent infection. On a previous occasion, I got a few quills in my ankle but I was at fault, getting too close to the porcupine. Since then, I stay at least five meters away from this prickly creature.

Waterton Lakes National Park is an animals' realm. Nowhere else in the Canadian Rockies in a small area like this cozy park could one find so many species and numbers of animals. Summer is comfortable everywhere but winters are not. Waterton is blessed by an almost continuous warm wind called a chinook, which keeps snow down and temperatures up. This is why animals find good winter pasture and love it here.

One nice, warm, late summer day, I climbed up to Carthew Mountain and bivouaced right on the summit. Incredible scenery and animals everywhere. On the way up by Summit Lake, a large sign said: "Grizzly in the area." Next morning, I got up before the sun and waited to witness that glorious sunrise over the prairies. The sky was clear and the temperature quite warm ($-5°C$), considering the location. In the dim light, I could see way below me, by Carthew Lakes, dark silhouettes of animals moving in different directions, some to drink water, others going to their favourite pastures and meadows. The sun was still minutes away so I sat and delighted in this great animal kingdom. Gentle sounds reached me from behind and, from the west-dark side of the mountain, a small band of sheep emerged. They could not see me sitting behind the boulder so I watched them coming and lamented to myself that it was too dark to photograph. Suddenly, like being hit by lightning, the sheep took off, virtually flying. I thought that my beard frightened them. I could not see or realize what had happened. I stood up and had a better look. I saw a medium-sized creature with a bushy tail walking slowly down the dark side of the mountain. And the sheep? It took them merely 30 seconds to run down to the mountain base, which would take me one hour to do. They simply flew over these incredibly craggy north ridges. They never stopped, running down to Carthew Lake and continued, not taking any chances. And what about the sad, disappointed predator who narrowly missed its breakfast? While I waited to photograph my sunrise, nearby behind the boulder, a wolverine waited for that flock of sheep. The sheep did come along its way, but when attacking one young sheep, the agile mountain acrobat jumped up right to the sky, alerting all the sheep and sending the flock flying. The wolverine went empty-handed. This incredible incident, witnessed from just a few meters away, assured me how fortunate I was. I took photos of the gorgeous sunrise, happily scanning the endless horizon, recognizing many mountains and then slowly went down to my tent and had a delightful hot oats and peaches breakfast. And what about the poor wolverine? Hopefully, the next morning, something would come his way.

On a warm, sunny summer day, I wandered along the Fraser River in Robson Park. By Overlander Falls, I noticed a group of kayakers above the falls. They had just portaged their kayaks to avoid the deadly spot, but, to my surprise, one kayak went straight down toward the falls. The water flows so fast that I barely had time to catch this kamikaze on film (plate 104). He went through that angry, boiling water like magic, right on the surface. Encouraged by this the next kayak went down. This one, however, had less luck and from the beginning, went straight under the water and disappeared. We counted 50 long seconds and some people said that he is in big trouble. Two rescue kayakers positioned below the falls looked nervously for any sign of him, but to no avail. It was five seconds later when a paddle emerged from the water and floated downstream, two seconds later, the kayak emerged in another spot but upside down and drifting lifelessly. The rescuers panicked, the people on the shore stopped breathing. It was unbearable to realize that the life of a young, husky fellow had been claimed by the mighty Fraser. From then on, seconds dragged like hours. We all realized that we witnessed a tragedy, that mighty nature most often wins. At 62 seconds, a red helmet emerged two meters from one of the rescuer's kayaks. Friends rushed and grabbed the nearly drowned man and got him out of that deadly water. The guy got some water inside but miraculously coughed it up and could manage on his own after some rest and help from friends. Why did he spend 62 seconds down under that murky water? The whirlpool kept him turning around and around. Finally, realizing that he couldn't get out of it, he freed himself from the kayak by undoing the safety harness and swam out of that whirling water to the surface. Now, you try not to breathe for 62 seconds. If you make it for 45 seconds, you are good, but under the water, it is more difficult because one does not breathe through the body. To celebrate their friend's survival, two kayakers who watched the drama from the cliff jumped spontaneously into that icy water.

So, we do have one of the most spectacular wildernesses of them all, the Rockies. Five National Parks within these mountains guarantee nature's safety and health. What more do we want? Well, as we all know, there is never enough of anything. Naturalists would turn more areas into National Parks; industrialists would log, mine, develop anywhere. We must strike a sound, intelligent balance which will satisfy all. Any exploitation of minerals or logging in a sensitive environment brings only short-term gain and long-term destruction of flora and fauna. It would take up to 70 years for fragile mountain vegetation to recover, for example, after open-pit mining. Fauna, however, once destroyed is gone. In my humble opinion, the entire Rockies from Waterton to Liard River should be declared as a wilderness reserve with very limited development. Why not create a great, clean, healthy industry —tourism on a gigantic scale? And tourism is a very economically sound industry. Imagine, when some countries cut down their last tree, polute to death their last river and lake, we would have something very precious to offer these people. People from around the world would flock here to see elsewhere extinct moose, bear, bald eagles or just the plain crow. There are countries on this planet where in the next 30-40 years, there will not be one single wild animal left. Industry, in some senses, brings a higher standard of life, granted, but certainly it lowers quality of life very drastically. What is the use of having two cars when there will be nowhere to travel? Everywhere will be a big, polluted, noisy city with California-style traffic jams. Wouldn't we be better off, rather, to decrease our population and expand our wilderness areas? Wouldn't it be a splendid idea to create along the southern Alberta foothills, a

Rocky Mountain Wildlife National Park, some 50 × 20 km., and have ten thousand buffalo there, along with elk, deer, antelope, moose and others roaming free? Wow! The world would come to see it and would be amused. The only problem is how to get our dear politicians interested. The moose or buffalo would not vote for their party or pay back favours for the contract. Perhaps we, the people, must demand these things from our government. Over a hundred years ago, there was a concerned man of wisdom and vision, who said: "In wilderness is the preservation of the world." Yet, a hundred years back, there was hardly any heavy industry, pollution or danger to wilderness, but Henry David Thoreau blew the whistle—he knew what was coming.

Today, we have a damaged ozone layer, global pollution, badly contaminated oceans. Cancer is devastating the population because of food and water contamination, senseless tobacco smoking and constant stress related to our "modern way of life." All that does not alarm too many people yet. We are told that this is the way it goes and we must drink one little sip of water from a disposable plastic cup; we must use disposable electronic items, cameras, cloth diapers, etc., and produce mountains of garbage. Most products on a store shelf are in large boxes almost half empty inside. Why? Because the producer wants you to believe that you are getting a lot for only $9.99, and you, the consumer, pay for this half-empty box. Now, we must cut almost twice as many trees to produce these large half empty boxes, which will have to be burned and create twice as much pollution. We could recycle these boxes, but it is cheaper to cut down a tree than recycle paper. So our god the dollar makes it legitimate to ravage, devastate our green lungs, the forest until there will be no more trees to cut. And then what? Fortunately, we do have a large number of wise people and organizations who knows very well what is happening to our wilderness and environment and who the culprit is. Let's support these people in any way we can, and when elections come, ask your candidate where he or she stands on environmental issues. Let's save our planet, our country, our Rockies from overpopulation, overdevelopment, pollution and destruction. We must keep the Rockies green, healthy and beautiful. Let's keep the Rockies as they are—The Living Rockies for the benefit and enjoyment of us, and the next generations.

The Author

GEORGE BRYBYCIN is a passionate enthusiast of nature, wilderness and mountains. The Rockies are his home, where he spends most of his life exploring, photographing, admiring and learning from nature.

Born and educated in Poland, George has travelled and explored natural wonders around the world; climbing mountains solo is his speciality.

His sensitive, artistic nature and the talent to see beauty reflects so obviously in his photographs.

With this publication, George celebrates the fifteenth pictorial book he has produced to date and promises many more to come.

George's books are not just pretty pictures. His writings and photo captions always have a message. He informs and entertains but preservation and protection of nature, wilderness and, in general, the environment we all live in are his paramount concerns.